Magnolia Fawn

By Paula Richey and Connie Hall

Written by Paula Richey and Connie Hall
Illustrated by Paula Richey

www.OtherRealmStudio.com
OtherRealm Studio
1150 Hayes Drive
Gray Court, SC 29645
ISBN 978-1-958396-07-0

The Carolinas' wilderness is home
to many whitetail deer that freely roam
between the subdivisions' fenced in tracts.

Before development, deer held sway.
With fewer wilds for deer to go or stay,
remember how to lessen our impacts.

Be careful, for deer do not understand
that roads, unsafe to cross, divide the land.

As one, the herd will migrate place to place.

They roam at dusk and chilly early day
to leap and bound across the country lanes
to follow after white tails like a race.

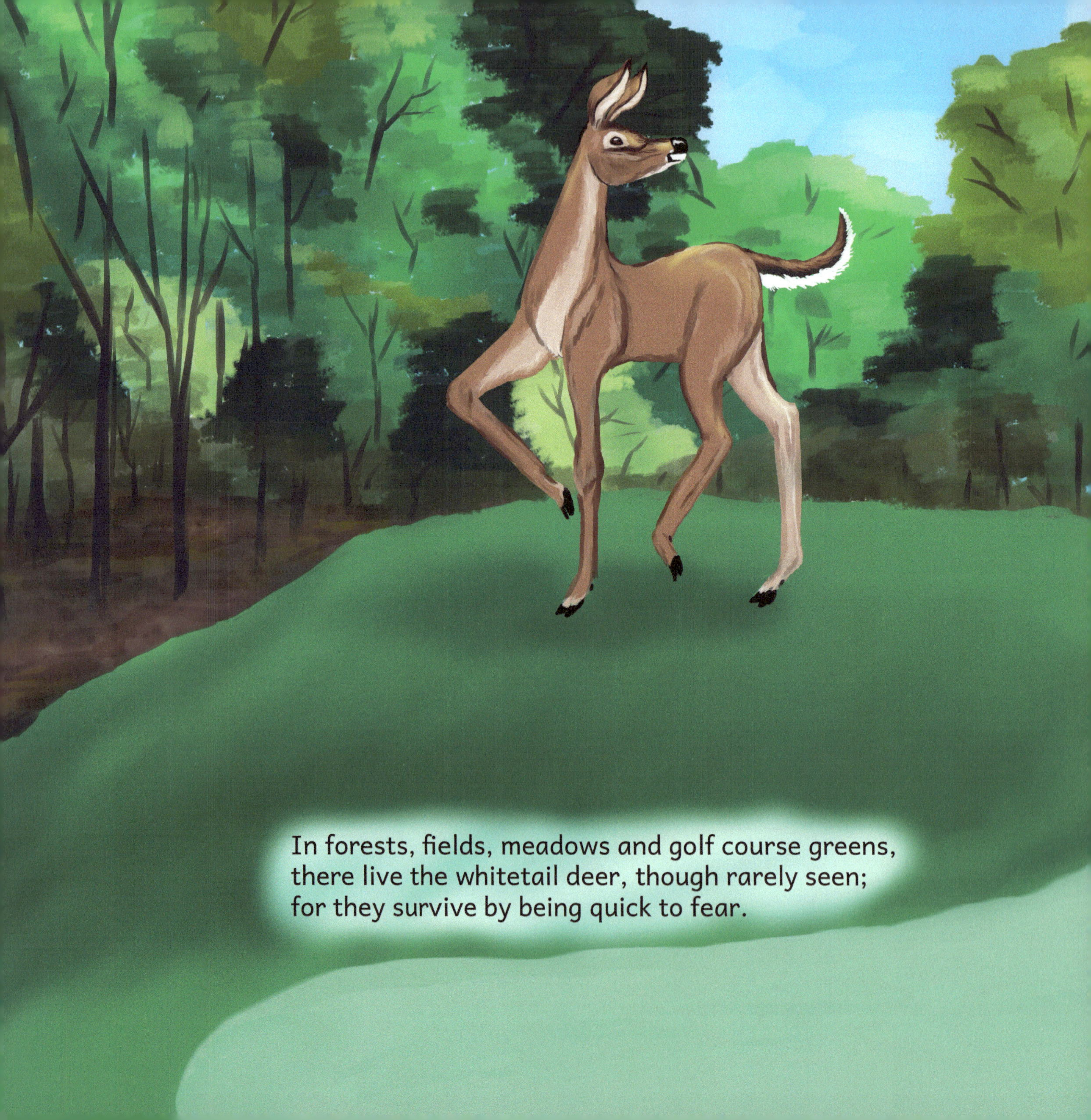

In forests, fields, meadows and golf course greens,
there live the whitetail deer, though rarely seen;
for they survive by being quick to fear.

In fallow fields of still and silent dawn
a mother doe will hide her quiet fawn
to wait in secret while she grazes near.

The baby deer, concealed in grasses, lies,
As hour after hour passes by.
The fawn is fine, so leave it safe alone.
The mother doe will likely soon return.
If there's danger or if you're still concerned,
then get your state's DNR* on the phone.

*DNR: Department of Natural Resources

An orphan's needs can be misunderstood.
Improper care does much more harm than good.
For fawns are delicate, easily ill.
Their lives are prone to unforeseen mistakes,
that even those with good intentions make.
Rehabbers will have medicine and skills.

Among the states' responsibilities
are lists of volunteers with expertise.

Magnolia Fawn is Connie's own land,
her rural charity for whitetail deer.
Among the hundreds rescued every year,

of fawns she's warmed and fed
and helped to stand,
some fawns are orphaned
young by accidents,
or caught in tangled wire
or trapped by fence.

If fawns are injured, crippled and alone
Magnolia Fawn will take these orphans in
until released into the wild again
so they'll be wild and free when they are grown.

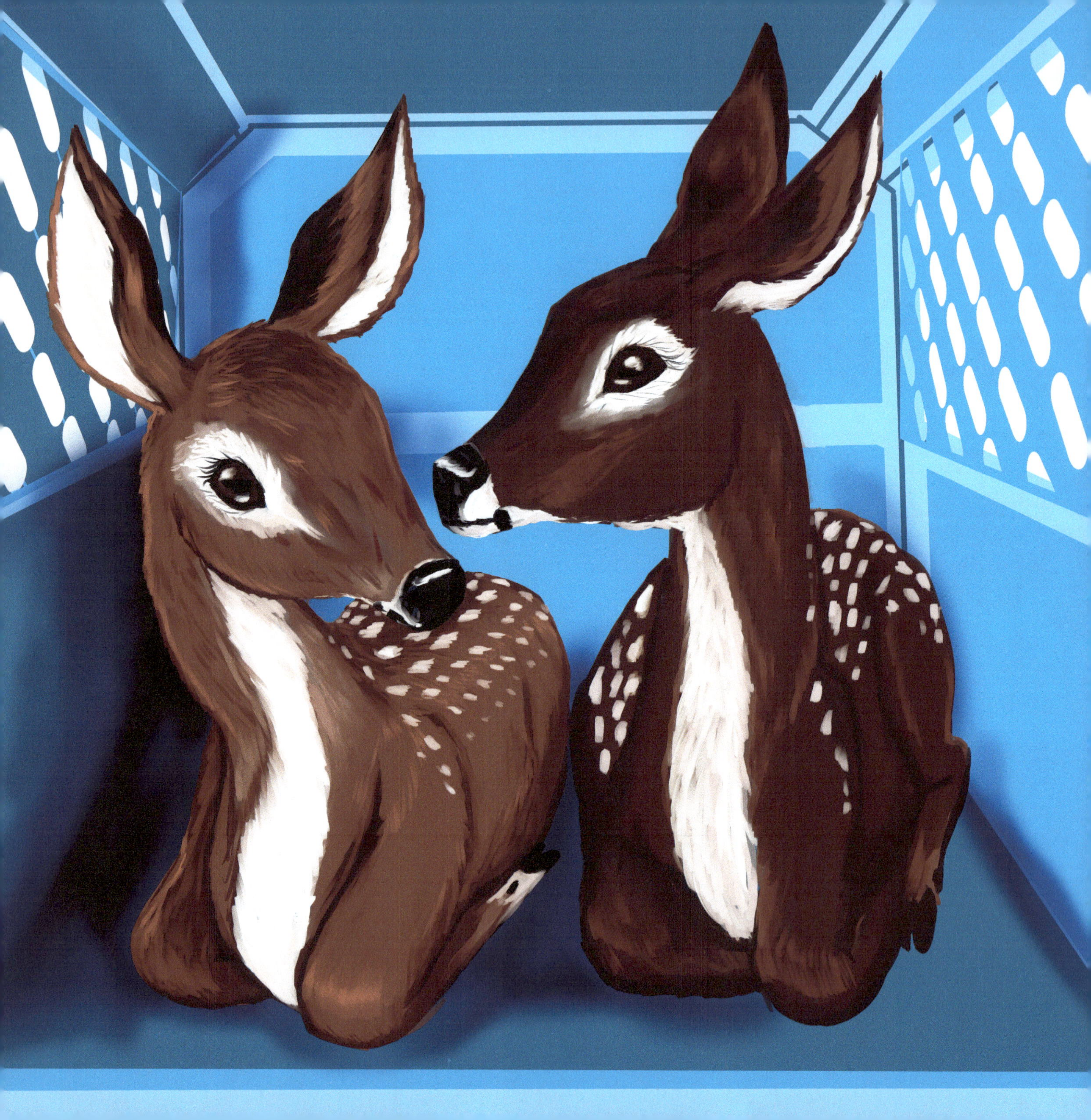

Since fawns are young
and so innocent,
They must never be
allowed to imprint
on humans, taking
care of them when small.
Or else will grow up
into problem deer
That seek out people,
lacking healthy fear,
and haven't learned
to live as deer at all.

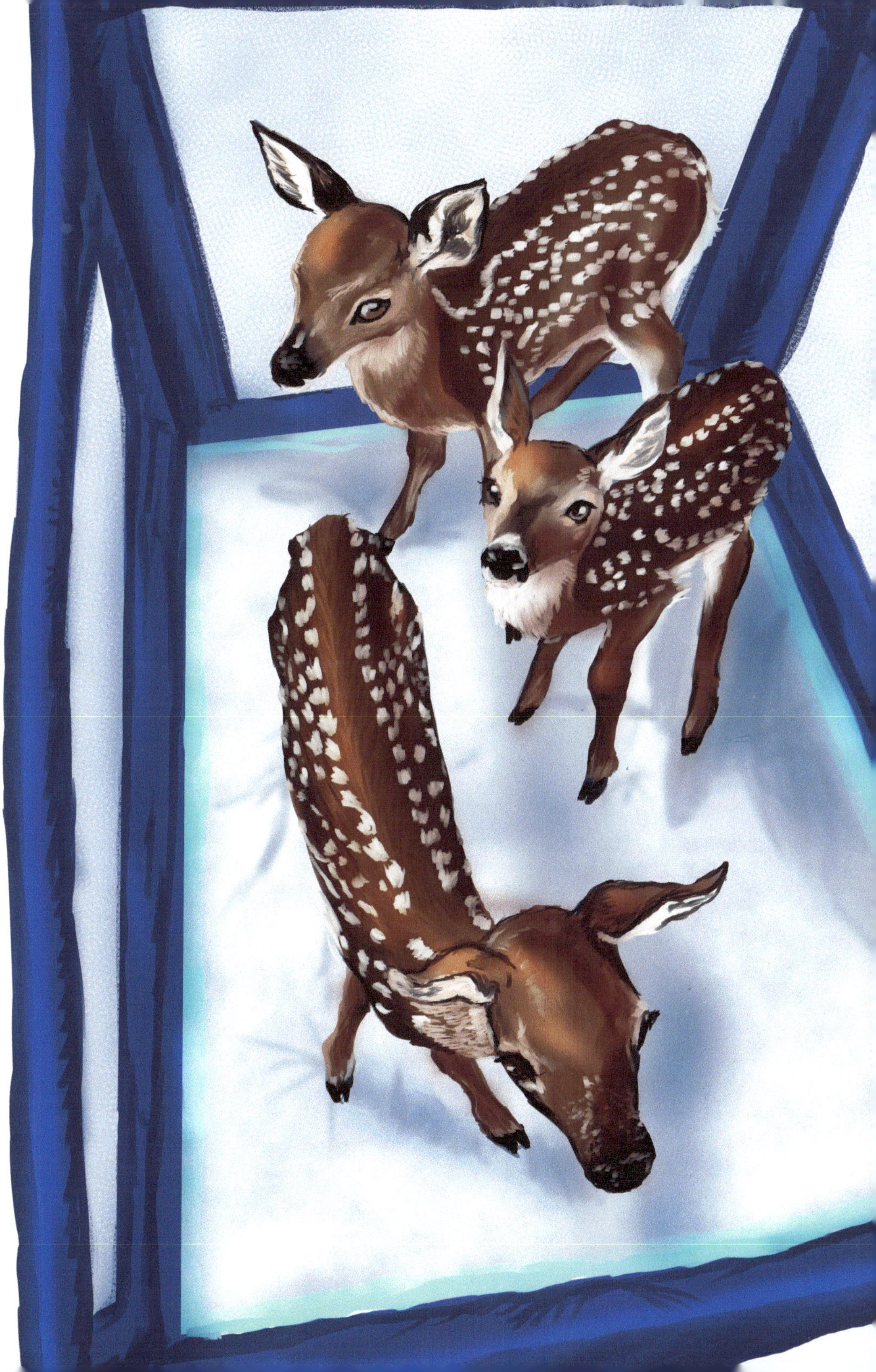

To raise a single fawn
is out of norm.
Here, they're together,
and a herd is formed
which once were orphans,
now none are alone.

When they all leave here, they'll be well prepared
to live their lives and tend their own welfare
the way they should have lived, wild all along.

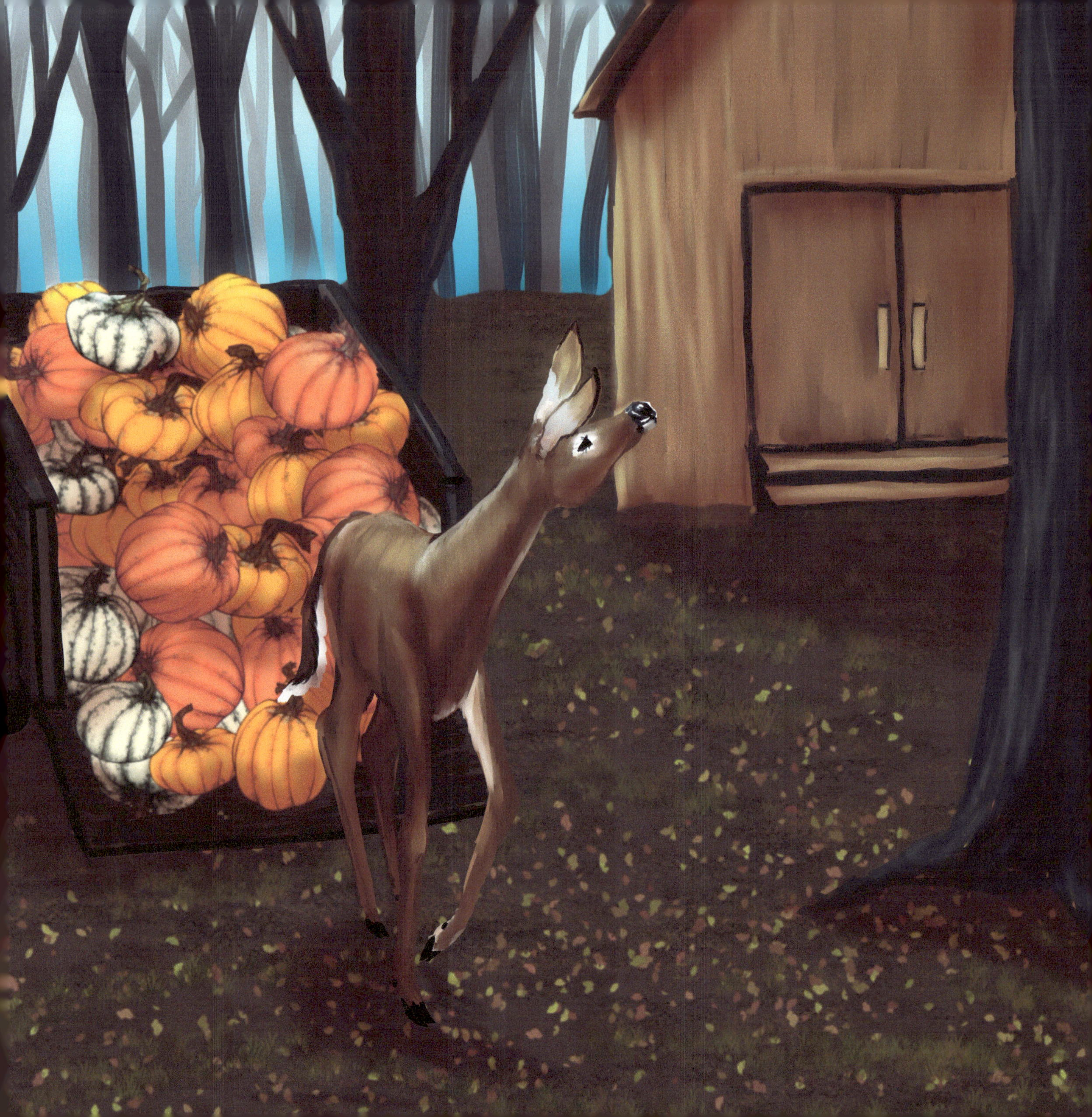

Although, not every fawn
can be set free.
Like piebald dwarfs,
the blind, and amputees,
and former pets,
now too unwary grown,

And others which may not survive as wild.
All need a place, so once permits are filed,
they stay in Connie's sanctuary home.

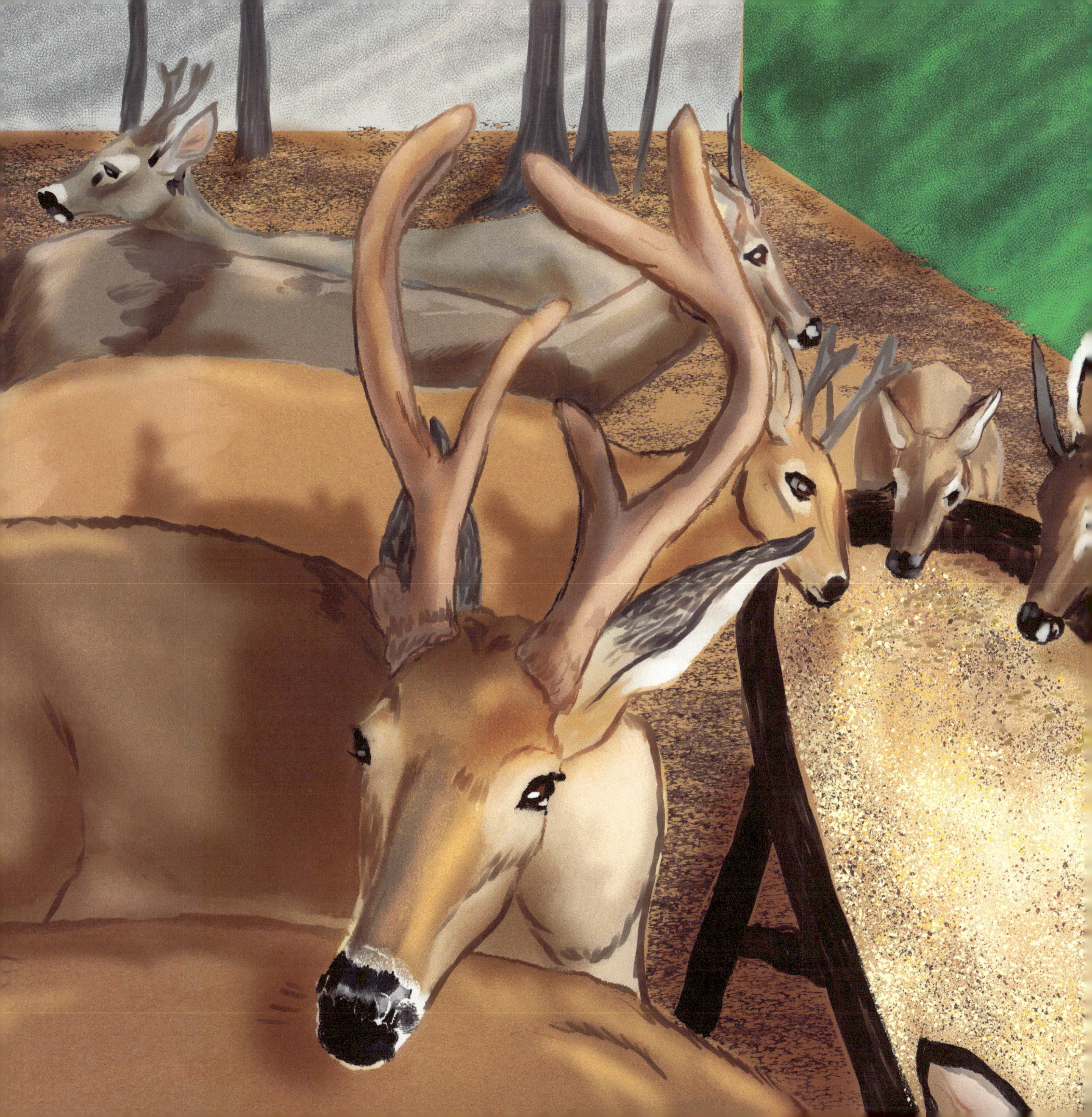

Magnolia Fawn Rescue is a 501c3 nonprofit that gives orphaned and injured whitetail deer fawns a second chance at life. You can help Connie save the fawns by donating or volunteering!

Visit magnoliafawnrescue.com to learn more and get your free printable coloring pages.

Also, you can follow @MagnoliaFawnRescue on various social media sites to see pictures, videos, and updates about all the animals at Magnolia Fawn Rescue. https://linktr.ee/Magnoliafawnrescue